KELLY RIPA BOOK

The Biography of Kelly Ripa

University Press

CONTENTS

INTRODUCTION

Kelly Ripa's striking blue eyes, charismatic personality, and willingness to be open and honest have combined to make her one of America's favorite celebrities for over three decades. She has been interested in acting since childhood and achieved Hollywood success early and often. Her first role was in the famed soap opera, All My Children. During this time, she met Mark Consuelos, the man she later married in 1996. She played a character named Hayley Vaughan, and worked on the long-running show from November 1990 until December 2002, then appeared for a couple of episodes in early 2010 when the show celebrated its 40th anniversary. She proved to be every bit as much a charismatic character as she has shown in her role as a daytime host. It didn't take long after she joined the show to become one of its most popular characters.

However, when Kathy Lee Gifford left *Live with Regis*

and Kathy Lee, Ripa stepped into a role that helped cement her name in both Hollywood and the media. For the next decade, she worked alongside the legendary Regis Philbin. The two had an interesting and playful dynamic that kept audiences coming back. Philbin finally decided to retire in 2011, and Ryan Seacrest replaced him. This change proved incredibly beneficial to the show's appeal to a younger audience, giving the show new life.

Ripa has become one of the most powerful and influential people in media. She has worked in several positions both in front of and behind the cameras, earning her a reputation for being business-minded and a solid actor. Major politicians and celebrities sought to join her on *Live!*, demonstrating how she has acclimated to the host role, even after repeatedly expressing apprehension following Philbin's departure from the show. She has since taken on other roles behind the camera and moved into other industries. Like many other women, she became an entrepreneur and producer, giving her more control over the various aspects of production and her brand. She has been recognized with several major awards. Yet she has not sacrificed having a personal life. She has inspired many people with her social media posts showing a glowing relationship with her husband, Mark Consuelos. They have three children, and despite both she and her husband being former soap opera stars, they have managed to keep a positive relationship with the press.

CHAPTER 1

Early Life

O n October 2, 1970, Esther Ripa gave birth to Kelly Maria Ripa, the second daughter of Esther and Joseph Ripa. The small family lived in Stratford, New Jersey - a few hours drive from New York City. Her parents did not have the kinds of careers that would suggest both of their daughters would go into the field of entertainment. Joseph was a bus driver, and her mother was a homemaker. Joseph's more outspoken nature is a trait that his daughters followed, as he managed to take on the role of the president of his labor union. He had gone to college, attending the well-known Rutgers University. Her mother stayed home and raised her two daughters, giving both Kelly and Linda (her older sister) the stability that served as the foundation for their own families later in life. The children were raised as Roman Catholics, which was not surprising since their primary heritages were Italian and Irish.

Kelly's sister grew up to be a writer, putting them squarely in the entertainment industry, though with very different foci. Linda primarily writes children's stories. Joseph Ripa continued to rise as a leader, becoming the Democratic County Clerk for the family's home county of Camden, New Jersey, in 2009. Over the years, Ripa has talked about how close she was with her mother, particularly when she was growing up. Even writing to her mother in a book, "Growing up, I knew that I could count on your help for any obstacle that I faced. I could depend on you to drop off my homework at school when I left it at home, drive me around to all my activities, or even tell me my hair looked great when it was sprayed and teased to at least five feet in the air!" This relationship seems to have been a large part of Kelly becoming a doting parent later in life. Ripa's praise is somewhat surprising as her mother was pretty reserved about Ripa wanting to go into acting as a career. Despite that, Esther became very supportive when it was clear that Kelly was serious about making her career in the profession. Ripa later admitted that her mother was hesitant to support Kelly's goals because she was afraid that she would have her heart broken or be unable to make a living. Kelly understood her mother's hesitation and didn't hold it against her mother as she fully understood her desire to protect a child from both difficult fates.

Kelly Ripa showed an interest in acting and

performing from an early age. She took an interest in ballet when she was just three years old. Dancing remained a part of her interests until adulthood. It helped her get onto the small screen when she appeared on *Dance Party USA* when she was only 19. Her interest in acting started to gain more traction when she began acting in high school plays. Cathy Parker, an agent, saw one of the high school plays in which Ripa performed, *The Ugly Duckling*. She even approached the high schooler to encourage her to continue as an actor, seeing that there was some talent that could work for the teenager. Ripa continued with her time at Eastern Regional High School until graduation. Still, she took the idea of becoming an actress seriously as she entered adulthood. Her drama teacher also encouraged her to keep going at acting, which must have boosted her confidence about her potential future career.

Ripa listened to Parker (and Parker remains her manager today), and she decided to go to Camden County Community College with a focus on acting when she could. She was working toward a degree in psychology but decided that it wasn't the direction she wanted to take. Instead, Ripa was more interested in seeing if she could find success in entertainment. With this in mind, she dropped out of college and moved to the Big Apple (New York City), a place known for helping actors find a career or showing them just how difficult it is. Since she didn't live too far from her home, she had more protection from the risks. After all, it would be easier to return home when it was just a few hours away instead of several states away from the city.

CHAPTER 2

All My Children

O ne of her earliest jobs after arriving in New York City was working as one of the demo girls who played with Nerf footballs at one of the city's toy stores. Her appearance on Dance Party USA was one of her first experiences in showbiz. Still, it wasn't quite along the lines of the career she was trying to have, despite having been a dancer for most of her life. She continued to appear on the show as a dancer, but she was looking for a role that had more substance. At first, she was interested in becoming a newscaster, thinking that being able to report the news and provide information to the public would be ideal for a career. In addition, being a newscaster would be much more stable than breaking into acting, which is notoriously difficult.

Ripa got her first big break in 1990 when she was

cast in the TV soap opera *All My Children.* She was only 20, making the casting of the part incredibly fortunate for the young woman. When asked how lucky she had been, she said, "There was never any clear-cut path. And anytime I tried to have a clear-cut path, that's usually when I would be disappointed. In the entertainment industry, you can only work so hard to achieve a goal. It's really 90 percent luck, 5 percent opportunity, and 5 percent skill." Ripa couldn't help but try to see how far she could go. If that is the case, it was a gamble that paid off in a way that no one in her family could have anticipated.

When she started her time on *All My Children*, Ripa played the character Hayley Vaughan, a teenager who appeared during Thanksgiving on the show. Her initial plot line had Hayley running away from home after the death of her father, and she was unwilling to live with her mother, who was an alcoholic. The character Trevor Dillon was her uncle, and Hayley decided to see if she could live with him instead of sticking it out with her mother. Her next major storyline was when her mother tries to take her back to Chicago, and Hayley fights returning to live with her. At the same time, Hayley is angry at a well-established character named Adam, who has hurt her uncle. Hayley claims to be his illegitimate daughter to one of the local papers to create problems for Adam. The plot twist was that she was his illegitimate daughter because her mother had had an affair with Adam years earlier. Her character also had a somewhat tumultuous relationship with a boyfriend in high school and her early adulthood. When she wouldn't be intimate with him, her boyfriend marries someone else, apparently breaking Hayley's heart. She turns to alcohol and gets into a dangerous predicament that her ex-boyfriend saves her from. After having an affair with him, the couple learns that his wife is pregnant. The affair seems to end, and Hayley starts working to overcome her own alcoholism.

As expected, there is a lot of drama and intrigue around the character as she grows into a capable adult. Hayley doesn't have many relationships after that first one. Still, they are all problematic, including one where she leaves her fiancé at the altar on the day of their wedding. When hiding from her actions, she meets Mateo Santos, played by Mark Consuelos. Mateo convinces her to go back and talk to her fiancé and ask for more time. The couple eloped, but her mother started a relationship with Hayley's husband. After she and her husband split up, Hayley spends more time with Mateo. They grow closer and marry two years after Mateo enters her life. That was the marriage that lasted for Hayley. And some of the plot of the Soap Opera was mirrored by real life. Consuelos and Ripa became a couple throughout their time on the show.

After 12 years on the show, Ripa decided to move on to something else, knowing that the show had given her an unbelievable opportunity to choose whatever she wanted to do. When asked about it later in her career, Ripa enthusiastically said, *"All My Children* is responsible for my entire life. I don't like to say that lightly. I met my husband on *All My Children*. I had my children on *All My Children."* She continues to attribute all of her future successes to her time on the show because she was able to become established and develop a platform. In addition, playing a popular character on the show helped her to gain a positive persona in an industry where that kind of positive persona can significantly boost a person's career. Her continued recognition and thanks have also been viewed positively by the audience. However, the relationship with one of her costars became a bond that people who liked her would find particularly endearing.

CHAPTER 3

Joining Regis Philbin

R egis Philbin and Kathie Lee Gifford were one of the most popular daytime talk shows on American TV. Together, they turned morning banter into a program that people tuned in to watch every morning while they did their daily chores. However, Gifford decided to leave the show to pursue other interests, and she left her co-host position in 2000. Philbin continued to host the show on his own for a while as he and the show's staff looked for someone who could balance his boisterous personality. Many were brought onto the show to co-host with him. Still, he worked on his own for roughly a year before finally settling on someone untested in the arena of talk shows – Kelly Ripa.

After 12 years on *All My Children*, Ripa learned to develop positive relationships with her coworkers.

And she had remarkable chemistry with Philbin when she worked with him before officially joining the talk show. Philbin had been on the show since 1983, becoming the longest-running host on American TV. Still, fans of the show wanted to see him develop a rapport with another host like the one he had with his former co-host. Based on everything the studio and audience had seen, Ripa looked like the perfect solution. In his memoir published in 2011, Philbin talked about how Ripa had stunned him and the show's producers during her short stint as a guest. So they decided to bring her on permanently, even before she had wrapped up her time on *All My Children*.

Though it was announced that she would join in early 2001, she didn't leave the soap opera to help co-host the show until 2002. Ripa later indicated that her first day was an absolute whirlwind. While there had been some announcements within the show, it doesn't sound like it was widely known that she would be the permanent host – at least, that was the impression Ripa had during her first day. She said about 20 years later, "I don't think anybody was even expecting me to be the replacement host. It was really not a big announcement, it was just sort 'Oh! She is my new co-host,' and it was business as usual."

Having been on a set where everything she said and did was scripted, becoming a talk show host was an incredibly new experience. She later recalled that she felt entirely unprepared because there was no script, unlike *All My Children*. And whatever she said or did – as well as what Philbin said and did – was off the cuff. Being a guest who just had to be entertaining for a limited time was much different than having to be entertaining as a daily job. Suddenly, there wasn't a script, no directors were telling her what to do, and there weren't retakes. Initially, she felt she had too much autonomy and freedom to do whatever she thought of off the top of her head. She was only instructed to do or not do some things, such as mentioning that a guest had recently been arrested, a detail that those guests probably requested before agreeing to appear on the show. Apart from these bits of guidance, she was on her own to entertain the audience. One of the things that helped her to settle in and get comfortable with working on the fly was the recognition from Gifford herself. He had provided Ripa with encouragement going into Gifford's old role. With such a fantastic relationship with Philbin, Gifford felt he would know the best person to fill Gifford's old role. Having such a high vote of confidence from Gifford, as well as flowers, helped Ripa feel that she could get through the challenges of being on a talk show.

While there was definite on-screen chemistry between Philbin and Ripa, it was very different compared to the dynamic between Philbin and Gifford. Philbin was considered a grumpy host with a long legacy as a host. He couldn't have been more different than the bubbly, gregarious, youthful

Ripa. Their relationship became a bit more strained because Ripa was still figuring out what worked best for her. At the same time, Philbin was happy to keep things as they had been since it had worked so well for over a decade. The experience for the audience was definitely different compared to what the show had before Ripa. Still, the audience definitely approved of how the pair interacted on the show. The pair seemed to have a great rapport on-screen and were thought to be close friends.

Behind the scenes, their relationship wasn't quite so positive. When Philbin left the show in 2011, the way they said goodbye suggested they would continue to talk and exchange quips without the cameras. Unfortunately, this was far from the truth. Some of this was because they took a different approach to the show. Philbin preferred not to talk before the show, including not greeting each other. This was against Ripa's nature and experience. She and her costars had a lot of time off camera, so she had gotten accustomed to chatting with people even without the cameras rolling. There were times when Ripa said she had felt more like his mother, telling him to do or not do things, mainly for his own health. For example, after he had heart surgery, she tried to make sure that he was more careful of his health, eating and drinking better. There was even a time when she went into full mother mode, removing a splinter her co-host had gotten while the cameras were on and the audience was watching.

While they did not remain friends, even essentially losing touch by the time he died in 2020, they did seem to have mutual respect for each other. Ripa had no problem acknowledging that he was among the best storytellers she had ever encountered. In the entertainment industry, that is even more valuable than being talented in singing, dancing, or comedy because it kept the audience hooked until he wrapped up his story. Of course, it helped that he had been in the entertainment industry for about 60 years. But that didn't mean he would be good at it – plenty of people couldn't be as captivating as Philbin.

Philbin later thought Ripa took his departure from the show personally, feeling like he was leaving because of her. He then declared that he had left because he was 80 and was too tired to keep going. Ripa hasn't said what caused the rift between them. Still, even if they weren't talking to each other, there was clearly a lot of respect between them as they were very effusive and positive about each other in their memoirs. They both felt that the other brought the right attitude and entertainment on screen. In that particular industry, that can be very hard to find. Philbin said her talents were unique and unexpected, making such a difficult transition from acting to talk show hosting with little training or direction. When Philbin died, Ripa was one of the first to go online and mourn the loss felt within the industry without the long-time TV personality. She said, "We are beyond saddened to learn about the loss of Regis Philbin. He was the ultimate class act, bringing his laughter and joy into our homes every day on *Live* for more than 23 years." Whatever her relationship with him was like toward the end, her children adored Philbin. He had a great relationship with them when he and Ripa worked together.

Ultimately, she had a lot of respect for him. When asked about her opinion of him, she pointed to him as the reason for her success as a host, saying, "I think my biggest takeaway from the 11 years that I shared with him was that you have to be yourself. You cannot be one person on camera and a different person once the light goes off or the audience is gone. You have to be who you are." Considering they were two very different people, it is great to see that they worked through their different personalities to create a show that was incredibly popular for a long time, with Ripa proving to be just as entertaining in her own way as Gifford had been before her.

CHAPTER 4

The Big Screen

R ipa didn't immediately settle down into her role as a co-host. Instead, she continued a bit of acting work that followed her original career trajectory. Even though she was quickly accepted by the Live! audience, she was still looking for other work. She soon found that as a character on Hope & Faith. The show was about two sisters. The older, more responsible sister, named Hope Shanowski, is happily married and living with her family in the suburbs of Cleveland, and Faith Ford plays the character. Ripa's character is Faith Fairfield, a soap opera star who ended up getting killed off on the show she was on (Ripa's character Hayley was not killed off on All My Children). Unsure of what to do with her life, she escapes the spotlight by going to her sister's house, creating a lot of drama for the homemaker and her family. The show was a sitcom that ran from the fall of 2003 until spring of 2006, slotting into the TGIF comedy block on ABC. Joanna Johnson wrote the show. It was very loosely based on her time on the soap opera The Bold and the Beautiful (the name of the soap opera that Hope was fired from on the show was The Sacred and the Sinful).

One of the recurring characters on the show was Gary "the Gooch" Gucharez, played by Ripa's real-life husband, Mark Consuelos. Just like on *All My Children*, the pair were romantically involved on the show, but they had a much more tumultuous relationship than in real life.

The show was met with mixed reviews, and it never became a popular show. Over the three seasons, it was on the air, it steadily went down in the ratings, ranked #77 during the first season and ranked 103 during its last season.

Ripa has occasionally acknowledged the show and her role, particularly on social media. It demonstrates how she can have positive relationships with other actors after the end of the show. One of her recent posts showed her holding hands with Faith, her older sister and asking Faith if she remembered it. Ripa playfully says that she doesn't remember but is looking forward to seeing her costar again in the future.

Ripa has also remained busy as an actress while holding down her role on *Live!*, including taking on several voice acting roles. Often, she appears on a few episodes of other shows, such as joining *Ed* in 2022 as a recurring character and *Go, Diego, Go*. She had a more significant role in *Marin's Room* (1996) before she became a talk show host, hinting at the idea that she was considering becoming a movie star. She had a part in a few other movies before officially taking on her hosting role. After joining *Live!* she had a role as herself in *It's a Very Merry Muppet Christmas Movie* (2002) and *The Great Buck Howard*. Being one of the most popular morning show hosts has made it possible for her to do cameos as herself on TV and in movies frequently. This has allowed her to keep working as an actress – while not giving up her time on the show.

CHAPTER 5

Outspoken

R ipa is a talk show host inclined to speak out, even if her opinions aren't always popular. This is likely why people tend to like her. The former soap opera star is much more genuine and open about who she is, just as Philbin had recommended many years ago. Having taken his advice to heart, she tends to be very open with her audience about her opinions and perspective on life. Since becoming a household name, Ripa has had no problem using her very public platform to talk about issues that matter to her. She has largely said that she could only be so open and public about her views because of how supportive the show was.

During an interview in 2021, an interviewer asked Ripa about her role as co-host. She admitted that being in front of the cameras isn't her favorite thing and that for a long time, she has considered leaving

Live!. This is unique in the world of talk-show hosts because they usually keep the idea of leaving a show under their hats until they are ready to go. They also tend to have other jobs lined up before making any announcement.

The fact that Ripa isn't afraid to be open and opinionated has made her seem less personable than her bubbly personality on the show. This became particularly problematic after she started working with Ryan Seacrest. The two talked about being good friends before going on their show, so their chemistry and interactions likely mimic how they interact in person. Yet, when they started hosting in person, some viewers seemed to take umbrage with how Ripa talked to Seacrest. The viewers seemed to be very upset, and not too long afterward, they started expressing how much better he was at hosting the show. She had been on for more than 20 years (at the end of June 2022). Ripa took a break from the show, causing a lot of rumors to swirl about why she was absent. Seacrest himself has not said anything negative against his co-host, though. On the contrary, he has had nothing but effusive and positive things to say about her.

The timing of her vacation led to some speculation, especially as she has posted numerous pictures of her and her husband out having fun. At the same time, Seacrest continues to host the show with guests. So it does seem out of character for her to stay silent. However, it isn't entirely surprising, considering most people need a bit of a mental adjustment as people still struggle to return to what they were at the beginning of 2020. How open she will be upon returning to the show is still up for speculation. However, it is almost certain that she will continue to be outspoken for others when she thinks there is a reason to be. It is why Ripa has won numerous awards – she has used her platform to offer support to different groups.

CHAPTER 6

Philanthropic Efforts

Ripa has been associated with many different charities over the years. Some because people she knew and cared about were affected by the issues. Some because she wants to help others less fortunate. There is a relatively long list of charities and foundations that she has contributed to and has actively put forward, including on Live! The following are the causes that she has actively supported since she started acting on All My Children:

- American Heart Association
- American Stroke Association
- Breast Cancer Research Foundation
- Love Our Children USA
- Ovarian Cancer Research Fund
- Point Foundation
- Project Sunshine

- Stand Up For A Cure
- St. Jude Children's Research Hospital
- The Art of Elysium
- The Heart Truth
- UNICEF

She has been actively engaged in some of these charities, particularly the Ovarian Cancer Research Fund. This is a more personal cause because one of her friends was diagnosed with the disease. When asked about her work with the charity, Ripa responded, "I didn't know a lot about ovarian cancer. I educated myself, and my education came earlier than I would have liked when a friend of mine was diagnosed." Not only did Ripa spend time learning about the disease, but she also became an active advocate for the Ovarian Cancer Research Fund by becoming a spokesman for the organization. She has been one of their most recognizable proponents, even co-hosting their annual shopping event most years. She has talked about how the event has shifted from being primarily women to women and children as women would bring their kids to shop. Many husbands join in now, giving the organization more people to participate in charitable events. She has also hosted the Breast Cancer Research Fund events, particularly the Fashion Targets Breast Cancer event.

Another more personal cause for her is Mothers Against Drunk Driving because a drunk driver nearly killed her sister in an accident in 1999. Ripa once opened up about what the cause means to her based on her own personal experience, "Linda still walks with a limp – she will always walk with a limp. She has permanent nerve damage to her leg and in her foot." Since Ripa is close with her family, this is distressing because there is a constant reminder of just how close her family came to losing a loved one. This has motivated the *Live!* star; "I want to get the message across that it's not OK, under any circumstance, to have a drink and get behind the wheel of a car – ever. I am hoping to prevent a situation that alters the life of a family the way my family's life was altered." While they were lucky that the elder daughter survived, things will never be the same, and Ripa has felt compelled to highlight that people are likely to be far more drunk than they think they are. It is easy to feel that you haven't had too much alcohol, but it doesn't take much to impair someone's ability to react while driving. All it takes is one misjudged assessment of a person's abilities to result in a life-altering event, not only for accident victims but also for those who misjudged how impaired they were.

In 2001, before actually joining *Live!*, Ripa appeared on a celebrity version of *Who Wants to Be a Millionaire?*, hosted by Philbin at that time. She won $250,000, and her choice for the charity where the money should go was Tomorrow's Children's Fund. This cause provides financial assistance to parents with children diagnosed with cancer or other serious diseases.

One of the causes that have gained her the most attention is her efforts for the Point Foundation, founded to help ensure equal rights for people in the LGBTQ community. From co-hosting benefits to talking about it on *Live!*, Ripa has been recognized for her work for the foundation. When talking about the issue, she said, "I always say I feel like the live morning show is just my living room and I'm just having coffee. Being at these important events where it matters what I'm saying – it's to raise money, and you want to give people a good show but still get the message out there." In 2015, GLAAD honored her with one of their GLAAD's Excellence in Media Award. When she talked about the award on-air the next day, she confessed that she was more nervous about her speech because she didn't like public speaking. She went on to say that she could only have a platform to support the LGBTQ community because of how supportive the producers were.

It isn't just regular causes that she and her husband support. In 2020, she and Consuelos received a lot of attention for being very generous as the pandemic made life difficult for everyone, particularly children. The couple reportedly gave $500,000 to various New York City charities to provide stability for homeless families with children. By the end of the pandemic, they had given an estimated $1.5 million to help homeless children find stability and continue to get an education during a time when the only option was remote schooling. When asked about it, Consuelos said, "We realize how lucky we are – for all of us [he, Ripa, and their three kids] to be together like this is probably never going to happen again. This time has been so horrible for so many people." It is an interesting look into a family who both appreciates that they were able to be closer and have more time together while recognizing that many people were not in the same position – and that was why they were so generous during such a difficult time.

CHAPTER 7

Production Company

R ipa hasn't exactly been quiet about being uncomfortable in front of the camera, so it isn't surprising that she has opted to go into producing as a way of getting out of the spotlight. She and her husband started their own production company – a funny turn of events as she said she doesn't want to work with him daily on Live!. Then again, talking openly in front of the camera as a married couple is very different from working together as producers. As producers, their discussions are not available for constant speculation and assessment. Their company is called Milojo Productions. They have worked together behind the scenes just like they did in their early days on the soap opera, where they both got their start in the industry.

The production company, founded in 2007, is

headquartered in the city where the couple lives, New York City. The name is a combination of the first two letters of the first name of their three children, giving it a family connection for both of them. The company is small, with fewer than 25 employees. They focus on reality TV that is unique compared to many other types of reality TV shows. Their first offering was *The Streak*, about a wrestling team from one of the numerous Florida high schools that have managed to sustain a 34-year winning streak as of the documentary's release. The film was well received, earning an Emmy after premiering at the annual Tribeca Film Festival during the 2008 season. In addition, the documentary was played by ESPN for a wider audience, gaining a lot of attention for how it looked at the impressive run the school has pulled off for over three decades.

The success of the company's first efforts has gained them a considerable amount of attention. This has allowed the company to pull in several comedy writers with impressive CVs. This allows them to make some interesting documentaries and sell scripts that don't quite go in the direction the production wants to go. For example, they've sold scripts to HBO and ABC, including a musical comedy. They have also worked with several large companies, such as Lifetime, Bravo, VH1, E!, CMT, TLC, and Discovery.

The production company has a fairly extensive catalog. They have not stayed with a single genre –

though they do have a high number of productions on sports-related documentaries. The following are some of the best-known products from the company:

- *Dirty Soap* is a reality TV show that follows the lives of some of the best-known soap opera actors, bringing in the world where the couple met to the screen. It is an interesting look at one of the most melodramatic genres on TV.
- *Cheer* is a reality TV show that looks at how competitive cheerleading has become, following a team managed by coach Patty Ann Romero.
- *Secret Guide to Fabulous* is considered Reality TV. Still, it is broadly comedic as the hosts show people how to make most aspects of their lives fabulous, from the home to wardrobes to how to host a dinner party.
- *My Diet Is Better Than Yours* is about experts giving overweight Americans advice on losing weight using their unique diet and exercise program.
- *NewNowNext Vote Election Specials with Wanda Sykes*, which featured the renowned comedian and a member of the LGBTQ community. She talks about elections as a way to help educate and entertain viewers.

They also have some new shows, with Ripa hosting a game show called *Generation Gap*. Seacrest joins her for one show, adding another level of comedy as he and Ripa are decidedly less known among younger viewers. The show's premise is that families must work together to respond to questions one generation will know well. The twist is that the pair-up is usually grandparents and grandkids, meaning there is a vast difference in knowledge about things like pop culture and TV shows.

Going forward, the company seems to be moving into the true crime genre with a show called *Exhumed*. The show follows detectives who were able to solve crimes by exhuming victims, finding clues that were missed, or gathering DNA to help find justice for those victims. Milojo Productions has another true crime documentary focused on the life and mystery around Cari Farver. The documentary's title is *The Disappearance of Cari Farver*. The actual events are unbelievable. Especially when one considers the lengths to which the murderer went to try to hide what she had done and how her actions caused significant harm to four families. It is a real-life story that leaves people feeling paranoid and in disbelief.

The company also has plans to make a thriller called *Mexican Gothic*, adding another genre to the company's catalog.

CHAPTER 8

Live!

Her casting on a morning talk show was a complete surprise, even to Ripa, as she had never considered taking that career path. Still, it has proven to be an incredibly well-made decision. Though she has gotten the flak for being outspoken, she has been the steadying hand on the show as she has continued to host for over two decades. She took over as the host following Philbin's well-deserved departure.

So far, she has lasted longer than two of her co-hosts, Philbin and Michael Strahan. Some people have criticized her for her reactions to their departure. However, it is important to understand how she learned that she was losing both of her co-hosts. Philbin didn't think that they should talk before the show started, so they didn't have much interaction before the show began. After 28 years of hosting the show, Philbin announced his retirement in January 2011, letting people know that his last day on the show would be that summer. However, that date got pushed back to November 18 since people wanted to plan a special goodbye for the show's long-time host. While he had been working on planning his exit with the producers, no one told Ripa that he was leaving until 15 minutes before they were on air. This gave her little time to process and comprehend the incredible shift in her responsibilities as she would become the sole host. She had been on the show for over a decade. Still, it seems unfair that many people knew and excluded her from the planning as it had the most effect on her work and responsibilities. It is understandable why she felt his decision to leave might have been because of her since she had been intentionally excluded from future planning of the show. By contrast, Gifford had told Philbin she was leaving the show a few days after making her decision, making him one of the first to learn of her departure.

Strahan replaced Philbin as the show's co-host in 2012. He had a different background, coming out of the sports world after having been a defensive end for the New York Giants. He cut his teeth as a host when he became an NFL commentator, giving him some experience in the role, though it wasn't quite the same as a morning talk show as the focus was not on sports. He had joined Ripa on the show about 20 times in the 2-year search for Philbin's replacement, and the two seemed to have great chemistry on air.

He co-hosted with her for four years, then – like Philbin – he worked with the producers and others behind the show to plan his exit so he could join *Good Morning America*. But, again, the news was withheld from Ripa until he was ready to announce it to the audience. He later said of what has been reported as a tense relationship between them, "One thing I tried to do is have a meeting every few weeks with her. We met a few times, and that was fine. But then eventually she said she didn't need to meet. Can't force somebody to do something they don't want to do." He seemed to fault her for not wanting to meet to plan the show, after Philbin had made it clear he didn't even want to talk unless the cameras were rolling. Neither man felt that she needed to be informed about their departure, despite it being a significant change in her role. It would mean she would be hosting the show alone while looking for a new host. And she was expected to do that with far less warning than many other people on the show.

When Ripa learned that Strahan was leaving, she took a week off, making it clear she wasn't happy about the turn of events. Her relationship with her second co-host was said to have been less than favorable, though it did not show on-screen. It is easy to see this planned departure as something personal even though the people behind the show said they were trying to negotiate moving him to another show carefully. He was asked to join *Good Morning America* and felt it was time to leave *Live!*. Perhaps it is ironic that Philbin actually spoke up for Ripa, saying he could understand why she was upset.

Following Strahan's 2016 departure, Ripa's friend Ryan Seacrest took over the host role. Many have speculated that the way new people can easily slide into the roles on the show without hurting its ratings is a sign of just how adept Philbin was at creating a fantastic show that could be successful as long as there was good chemistry on-screen. It seems to work better with friends on-air than hiring someone less familiar with their co-host.

As of 2022, Ripa has been on the show for over two decades, making her the second longest-running host. There has been recent speculation that she is considering leaving the show, especially after she recently took a long vacation with her husband. Between the production company and a clear desire to have more personal time, it would make sense. However, as of August 2022, she is preparing to return to her role after taking an extended break.

CHAPTER 9

Personal Life

Her recent images from her vacation show Ripa is perfectly happy with her personal life, even though she and her husband recently became empty nesters.

Ripa is the ideal type of celebrity because of her numerous philanthropic efforts. Still, her personal life is equally something that people point to as life goals. Her relationship with her husband is an example that people point to as what a good marriage should look like. Both of them had discussed their initial reaction to the other, with Consuelos saying that he knew she was out of his league when they met, indicating he didn't think that she would ever consider him a romantic interest in real life. However, Ripa had a completely different takeaway from her first impression of him. "I saw my husband in a photograph before I saw him.

And I knew when I saw his photograph." Indicating that she knew she would marry him even before she met him.

Like their characters on the show, there was some drama between the couple behind the scenes. Years after they married, Ripa admitted, "Right before we got married, we broke up. We broke up and got back together the day before we went off and eloped. Yeah, we eloped. We went to Vegas and got married." They had dated for a year, then took a break from each other. They were then asked to be on *Live with Regis and Kathie Lee* because a mom who had dreamed of meeting the soap opera couple was appearing on the show. Consuelos admitted that Ripa's not talking to him while they were filming and that "made me go crazy, so I followed her into Central Park... and we got married the next day." When the couple decided to get back together, he proposed. They headed off to Vegas the next day to make their reunion more permanent. Much later, Seacrest asked her on the show about the experience, and she admitted that she thinks that getting eloped made it easier to tie the knot: "We just had a very normal, very regular wedding. It is such an efficient way to get married. And it was fun. We were like, 'Now *this* is gambling! Woohoo!'" Her initial response may have been joking, but she told her co-host that she thought they wouldn't have made it to the wedding if they had been forced to go through the usual wedding planning. As she was glowing about her relationship, Seacrest expressed that he wasn't sure about marriage (he's never been married). She was eager to let him know that his opinion was fine by saying it was not for everyone. She said that she thought they had been successful because they met when they were young enough to be malleable for each other. They learned how best to work together more functionally before they had a lot of relationship baggage that could have made communication and interactions more difficult. Yet they were old enough that they weren't likely to change significantly.

She had earned the reputation for being one of the strictest celebrities because when her kids were growing up, she insisted that they give up the passwords to their phones. They were also told they had to keep social media accounts private. She did not want them to grow up and feel entitled, so she strongly encouraged them to move to other cities and find their own ways without her and her husband constantly footing the bill. She was pleased when her eldest child finally seemed to learn the value of money, even just $20. They regularly received that amount for Halloween from their grandparents. Still, her eldest really valued it when he was paying his own rent and managing bills on his own. She quipped, "I think he loves the freedom. He hates paying his own rent and he is chronically poor." This seems to have been a hard-won battle with her kids, as the two eldest elected to go to school in New York City, where the family lives. She was far more adventurous and willing to make more significant changes in her life at their age. Ripa didn't move far, moving just a state away from her parents, but it was still a big change. The kids know that Ripa and her husband are there to help them when they need it, but they want them to find their own paths so they can build character and learn in a way similar to the lessons she and her husband learned.

Ripa and her husband are Catholic and have raised their children in their Faith. Ripa once talked about this with the magazine *Good Housekeeping*, telling the interviewer about her and her husband's thoughts on the matter, "We've both found it a stabilizing force, a source of strength and comfort in our lives. While we don't always say grace at meals, we do say our prayers every night." On occasion, they have even made appearances at charity events hosted by the church, including the Catholic Charities Brooklyn and Queens event.

She has been very open about her relationship with her husband, and it seems to be just as healthy and strong as it was when they met in the 1990s. Their most recent vacation in the summer of 2022 is a holiday that Ripa has happily posted about online. She enjoyed taking a vacation where it was just her and her husband. She admitted that it was the first time they could just get away together for a longer period of time without children or other family members almost since they became parents. As much as she loves her three children, she knows how to support and care for them and how to get out and enjoy life with her husband. It's in stark contrast to many celebrity couples who seem to grow apart as they age. It's part of what makes her so popular with her audience – she seems more grounded and relatable, appreciating what she has. After more than 25 years of marriage, the couple seems to be still happy and in love, even choosing to work together with their new production company. He has guest-hosted with her on the show a few times, and her whole family helped her keep filming during lockdown. Up to 2022, they seem to be a nearly perfect family willing to step in and help each other.

CHAPTER 10

Beloved

While most people in the media are considered polarizing figures, Ripa has mainly remained popular because of her bubbly personality and willingness to talk about many different topics. Some people have accused her of always bringing the subject back around to herself, but that is true of most (if not all) talk show hosts. They talk about their lives for the entertainment of their audiences. And many of the people who tune in to watch Live! enjoy hearing a woman talking more bluntly about her life, highlighting things that are incredibly relatable to the viewers. She comes across as being very relatable and friendly. She also very readily admits that she has really lucked out, which comes across as being humble, saying that there are a lot of reasons why she has been successful, and a lot of that was out of her hands.

Even with the drama behind the scenes with her two previous co-hosts, she has always talked positively about them. They have been just as effusive about praising her professionalism and being incredibly good at her job. Her coworkers from *All My Children* have been almost entirely positive, talking about how they enjoyed working with her, both on camera and off. She and her husband were invited back to reprise their roles in 2010, a return they immensely enjoyed. She was incredibly sad to hear that the long-running soap opera was coming to an end.

She earned an Emmy for her time on *Live!* and has been recognized for her work with charities and communities. Ripa has been friends with Anderson Cooper for a long time, and he often joins her show as a co-host when one of the other hosts leaves, or someone goes on vacation. They are close, and he was the person to present her with the GLAAD's Excellence in Media Award in 2015. People who have worked with her often say that she is genuinely the person audiences see on the show daily. This is pretty impressive, considering the fact that she isn't a fan of public speaking or being in front of the cameras these days.

In 2022, she announced the release of her first book, *Live Wire: Long-Winded Short Stories*, a memoir of her life up to 50. Ripa has said it took her 18 months to write it, but it was a labor of love. It is a different view since most celebrities choose to hire a ghostwriter to do much of the heavy lifting. Ripa actually wrote the book herself, which she explained was why it took her so long. Her self-deprecating humor will likely come through in the book as she has deployed that type of humor in trying to market her book. When she finally showed off a copy of the book on *Live!*, she joked with Seacrest that she was hoping people would think that Sarah Jessica Parker was on the cover so that people would be more likely to buy it. Though she has talked about many aspects of her life on air, she seems to have at least a full book of stories to tell in her book. At the time of writing this book, she is supposed to return to the show. But, at the same time, she plans to go on tour to promote her book following its release in September 2022.

CONCLUSION

Kelly Ripa has become an iconic member of morning talk shows. She can be energetic and bubbly, even during difficult times. Starting life in New Jersey, nothing about her early life suggested that she would go into entertainment. Even early in her career, it wasn't easy to tell where she would go with her talents. However, after guest hosting with the legendary Regis Philbin, it became clear that she was a nearly perfect fit for daytime talk shows because of how friendly and entertaining she was with the long-time host.

All celebrities have their detractors, but Ripa has remained well-respected. She can deal with negative comments and harsher criticisms without allowing them to upset her too much. Most of her audience thoroughly enjoys how she tells a story and invites them into her life to see her struggles. In large part, she has always wanted to keep from being altered too much by being a celebrity. She has also used her platform to help a lot of different charities and causes, particularly ones that have had a personal impact on her life. This willingness to help others has been part of why people have come to respect her and see her as the kind of celebrity who helps positively affect the world.

What is nearly as attractive to people is her very happy relationship with her husband after being married for 25 years. Pictures from the couple's first vacation showed that they both know how to enjoy each other's company in an entertaining, cute way, and sometimes a little more adult than what she can do on her family-friendly show. Her relationship with her husband is a large part of her appeal – they seem so happy despite being celebrities, which most people don't expect to see. Today, her openness and honesty continue to make Kelly Ripa a beloved and iconic public figure.

Made in United States
North Haven, CT
27 November 2023

44638752R00032